Story by Connie D. Mentz   Illustrated by Mike Beck

Dude FIERY
AND THE
GIANT
HOT DOG

A heartwarming parody of the world's favorite *tastemaker*

ULYSSES PRESS

Published by:
Ulysses Press
PO Box 3440
Berkeley, CA 94703
www.ulyssespress.com

ISBN: 978-1-64604-362-0

Printed in China
10 9 8 7 6 5 4 3 2 1

Editors: Renee Rutledge, Joyce Wu
Layout: Winnie Liu

Once upon a time, there was a guy named Dude Fiery.

Dude was many things: rad dad, classic rock fan, talented chef...

But most of all...

he was a lover of **bold** and **over-the-top** flavor!

Dude wanted to make the best-ever hot dog—a staple at diners, drive-ins, and dive bars.

Dude had eaten many a hot dog but wanted to turn the flavor **up to 11.**

He experimented day and night, until one day...

"Here," he said, offering a slice of Dynamite Dog to a villager.

"Not so fast," said a beige voice belonging to a somehow beige-er man.

"I am **Bartholomew Bland,** the Chancellor of Taste, and I determine the flavor profile of this town! No one can eat anything that doesn't follow the proper rules of taste and flavor, as determined by Taste Village regulations 5534, 122, Forms TAYS-T, TAS-TY..."

"This is **NOT** approved," huffed Bland.

And with one final sneer,
he marched away.

"Well, that was weird," said Dude. He took another look at the Taste Villagers munching away on their unseasoned chicken and salads.

"But clearly, there are more important things than the **Dynamite Dog** right now! These people need some **funky, off-the-hook** flavors. I better get to work!"

FLAVOR 101

Volcano Nuggets

Tear Spheres

Taste Grenades

Dude knew the best way to bring the heat to Taste Village was to get involved in the community.

His first stop: Taste Village Elementary School.

At first the teachers and kids were a little suspicious...

But Dude quickly won them over in the cafeteria.

In no time he had the lunch ladies, teachers, and kids creating the most awesome lunchtime meals ever!

"I'm onto something," Dude thought as he left the elementary school. "The way to these people's hearts is through amazing food."

TASTE VILLAGE ELEMENTARY

He only needed to convince the Taste Villagers to give him a chance. They were so used to the decrees of the Chancellor of Taste, but Dude was up for the challenge.

So, Dude went around town helping out wherever he could.

He stopped by the fire station to help
make dinner for first responders.

He stopped by the grocery store to suggest new tasty ingredients and help bag groceries.

He stopped by the hospital with sweet treats for all!

16

He baked an epic cake for an LGBTQIA+ wedding
and even stepped in to officiate!

Filled with love and good cheer that only a wedding can spark, Dude knew he could do even more.

He remembered the dull and boring Main Street and how there were several vacant storefronts.

Surely the people of Taste Village had some ideas on what could go in those shops, they just never felt like their opinions mattered.

"Let's fill these shops!"

Dude set up his hot dog booth. His new Taste Village friends were stoked to try the Dynamite Dog, and Dude was glad he'd worked so hard on making it absolutely packed with righteous flavor. But then, a shadow loomed over his counter.

"My main man Bart!"
Dude exclaimed.

"The hot dogs will be done in a few minutes.
I can't wait for you to try them!"

Bartholomew Bland glowered. "No one will be eating those hot dogs, Dude Fiery. This booth has not been approved by the Chancellor of Taste and is shut down."

And with that, Bartholomew Bland slapped a **"CLOSED"** sign on the booth.

CLOSED

Dude felt his heart drop. He was so amped to share his rad hot dogs with all of his new friends.

Heartbroken, Dude began packing up his mustards, ketchups, hot sauces, pickles, vegetables, and the rest of his condiments.

Maybe Taste Village wasn't ready for flavor-packed realness after all.

Just then Dude heard a small voice.

"Hey!"

Dude peered over the counter. The kids from the elementary school stared back. "Don't close your booth!" they begged.

More and more villagers gathered. "We want to try the Dynamite Dog!" they exclaimed.

"Dynamite! Dynamite!" they chanted.

26

The Chancellor of Taste, unable to ignore such a huge crowd, began second-guessing his hasty decision to shut down the funky-flavored booth.

"Come on, just try some," said one villager to Bland.

"Yeah, just one couldn't hurt!" cried another.

Dude eagerly began piling a mountain of rockin' toppings on the biggest piece of processed beef and pork Bland had ever seen.

Reluctantly, the Chancellor of Taste took one small bite.

"It's so...

TASTY!"

exclaimed the Chancellor of Taste, shocking Dude and every person in Taste Village.

"I never knew flavors like this could exist!"

And they all lived deliciously ever after.

Mike Beck is a designer and illustrator living in Black Rock, Connecticut, with his girlfriend, Dayna, and their two cats, Balki and Larry. He enjoys bad movies, dumb jokes, and fairly priced bourbons. Things that really make him laugh are watching people fall down and stupid animal videos. He is scared of clowns and a world without cheese.